AF413251

UPLIFTING POETRY DEVOTIONAL

BY
JANELLE MACKEY

DEDICATION

Dedicated to the brave souls who've endured hardship, to those who've lifted me up in my darkest hours, and to the memory of those who saw potential in me when I couldn't. Your belief in me made this dream a reality.

TABLE OF CONTENTS

ACKNOWLEDGMENTS

First and foremost, my deepest gratitude goes to the Heavenly Father, who bestowed upon me the gift and talent to create and share this book with others. His divine inspiration has been my guiding light throughout this journey. Secondly, I owe a profound debt of thanks to the cherished individuals in my life—those who provided help, encouragement, and motivation during times when my own strength, motivation, and confidence waned. Their unwavering support was a beacon of hope. Lastly, I am immensely grateful to the kind souls who haven't known me long but have blessed me with their kind words of encouragement and support. Their unexpected gestures of kindness have touched my heart deeply and sustained me through this process.

LOSING THE CARES OF THIS WORLD AND WORLDLY SYSTEM

What does it profit to gain the riches of this world and to lose your soul rather than to keep your soul and lose the world?

So many people get blinded by wealth and materialistic possessions and spend most of their time trying to achieve,

Success in this world isn't defined by how wealthy you are or how much you can show off.

In the end, your spirit, body, and soul aren't receiving the truth and reality of what the LORD can give you just by solely TRUSTING IN HIM,

When the HOLY SPIRIT wants to do a new thing in you or simply for you to receive salvation, the mind, spirit, and soul have to be reprogrammed by the reality of what the LORD JESUS says you are in HIM.

The blindness of the enemy has caused many to be deceived, looking to gain more in this world, and then stress, worry, fear, anxiety, and other spirits come to play tricks in people's minds, choking the word of GOD that comes to set them free,

The lust of this world and deceitfulness have caused many to hear voices and believe counterfeits of the enemy that think the LORD is behind a work or situation.

This worldly system is just a system of the enemy to trap you into believing you are bound and limited by situations and circumstances that won't change or there's no hope,

Truth is the kingdom of Heaven; the system from above gives life to your spirit, soul, and body.

The word of GOD strengthens, corrects, teaches, directs, and gives hope in any situation you're encountering,

The cares of this world only lead to death spiritually, but when walking in CHRIST, hope, blessings, peace, and reality give you a true life that this world can't give you.

COMING TO OUR HEAVENLY FATHER
OPEN AND FREE

There is liberty when coming to our heavenly Father,

For HE sees and knows all things.

Full of mercy, grace, compassion, and love,

We're able to go to HIM freely.

Be open and honest about struggles, dreams, and frustrations, and just talk to HIM,

Our heavenly Father knows the hearts of man.

HE sees hidden tears and fears,

HE wants us to come to openly and free.

To have the freedom to be honest and be open before HIM,

No matter what we think in our minds, HIS love for us never changes.

Instead of running from HIM, HE wants us to come with everything in our hearts, and by, HIS leading and word, HE shall lead and guide us in such a loving way.

DYING TO SELF

When walking and fellowshipping with the Creator of everything, there's a yielding and obedience that needs to take place,

It doesn't mean to do your own desire and pleasure.

Dying to your flesh means putting into subjection your body to be an instrument to the KINGDOM of GOD,

It means letting go of your plans, will, and agenda for HIS GLORY to be seen in the world.

It takes neglecting your dreams and heart's desire of what you want to do or achieve in order to see what the LORD wants to be done and accomplished in matter,

It's a form of humbling yourself, sacrificing, and completely surrendering everything to follow the HOLY SPIRIT'S leading and will in anything,

Dying to self is being selfless towards others to show the LOVE of CHRIST shed abroad our hearts.

WHEN WE WALK WITH GOD

It's a walk that's not always seen clearly through the natural eyes,

His ways are not our ways, but when things happen in our lives, we get surprised.

Sometimes, it costs the stuff we love and desire for his will to fully take place,

When walking with God, everybody may not comprehend your calling, but He is faithful to bring events to come and pass in our lives.

We start to lose people, possessions, and friends in this world but gain more from God,

The more we walk with God, the more of his blessings, peace, promises, and open doors we have from HIM,

This walk with him costs us our will, passions, and paths for our lives so we can see His true will and paths for our lives.

THE GOODNESS OF GOD

His love for us can never be shaken or moved,

He is faithful and just despite the mistakes we make.

His eyes are ever towards us day and night,

When bad things happen in our lives, he still never leaves our sight.

His word never ceases to come to pass,

His blessings, grace, and forgiveness are more than we think, so we should be thankful.

His plans for us are bigger than we ever think or expect,

Sometimes, when going through the wilderness, we feel like he left.

But He is a just God and Father teaching us to grow,

His Holy Spirit never stops dwelling in us as we allow His spirit to flow.

The goodness of God is too big to contain,

His power, promises, and blessings break every bondage and chain.

When He speaks to us, our hearts have the reassurance of His word,

The Goodness of God should be more appreciated and embraced,

Because the greatest love in life is his, and he never makes any mistakes in our lives.

THE DEPTH OF GOD'S LOVE

His hands are forevermore stretched to us,

His grace and mercy pour out no matter what we go through.

People leave our side in life, but He still remains there,

Situations spiral out of control in life sometimes, but somehow, miraculously, he brings us out of those situations.

The love of our Creator can't be imagined with the natural mind,

The depth of his love goes beyond the oceans, rivers, and seas.

Even when we doubt him, he still moves in our lives to make us believe in him more

This type of love can't be explained,

But, only if we just allow his love to come into our lives to be experienced more, we won't feel as alone.

IF THOU CAN KEEP THE FAITH

Dreams and visions come to us in our sleep a lot of times,

When our heavenly father shows us what's to come, why does doubt form?

Oftentimes, we doubt the plan the LORD himself has given us, but HE speaks to us in such ways.

When opposition comes, and others speak contrary to what we believed in the first place, the faith built up in the beginning dwindles based on outward opinions and thinking.

But, in the moments of opposition, hold still to the same faith, IF thou can keep the faith in what was shown in those dreams, visions, or prophetic utterances,

Mountains shall move, and the ones that doubted shall come to believe the LORD has done wonders.

IF thou can keep faith in the plan, will, and move of GOD, it shall manifest by FAITH what is going and supposed to happen,

Faith is the anchor and force that causes supernatural blessings, moves, and unseen situations to manifest wondrously.

BEING DECEIVED OF HEARING THE VOICE OF ANOTHER

Many false spirits have already gone into the world,

So many spirits are deceiving people.

The blindness and veil over people's eyes have caused the darkness of the enemy to persuade people to listen to false doctrines, teachings, and sermons that are not scriptural or mixed truth with lies of the enemy,

In these times, many teachings have gone forth to deceive, trick, or captivate people into thinking the LORD is behind a work or teaching when, in reality, it's a spirit of divination, deception, and or lying spirit.

Discernment to hear the voice of the enemy has to be increased,

False teachings are causing itching ears.

The voice of the enemy brings confusion, blindness, deceit, and nothing but chaos,

The spirit of the LORD brings joy, peace, love, and a sound mind.

Repentance in the mind is vital because it is a gateway for the LORD's word to change your thinking perception, and his HOLY SPIRIT shall guide you into all truth,

HIS voice shall lead you on the correct path to life and freedom in CHRIST.

The veil shall leave the eyes of people because there shall be no more deception,

Hearing the voice of another and being deceived causes spiritual darkness and being away from the BODY OF CHRIST,

Hearing the voice of the LORD shall make you come amongst fellow believers and know who you truly are in CHRIST JESUS.

DON'T PRAY AMISS

Praying to the Most High is communicating with HIM about emotions, wants, and needs and going to HIM with everything,

When praying for a certain situation to change to bring something needed or wanted, why do we miss it?

The prayers that were prayed got answered or are getting answered, but it's not sometimes packaged in ways not familiar to the natural mind or eyes.

The LORD answers in ways never dreamt or thought about,

We as a people question prayers answered that's in front of our faces.

Sometimes, we amiss based on our own desires and how we want to see the answer manifest,

It's in ways and forms of answered prayers from our Creator that make us question how prayers are answered in unfamiliar ways, but in reality, it is the answer that is given.

WAITING PATIENTLY WHILE STAYING THE COURSE

Walking on the path that Most High has you to stay on can get lonely,

Sometimes, patience runs thin.

But, in the moments of asking questions and trying to figure out the next move of the LORD, just wait patiently,

While staying the course, your faith shall be put to work and in use.

The physical eyes can make you doubt in your mind that the LORD is not moving, but it's in those moments of waiting, persevering, and staying focused on the course ahead that cause more trust, gladness, and to see how the Most High is moving,

It doesn't matter how the physical circumstances and situations look; keep trusting, waiting patiently to see the goodness and grace of GOD take over.

OUR CREATOR LIVING INSIDE US

Being born again means coming into this life of inheritance, blessings of Jesus Christ,

The eyes are no longer blinded by the deception lies of the enemy.

When being saved, the Holy Spirit himself comes into our hearts to dwell on,

HE guides, leads, speaks, and directs our steps.

He breathes in us true life,

As we walk in life, he is there leading and teaching us more.

Our Creator is ever present in our lives,

When He dwells in us, he is shaping and molding us to be,

That's the beauty of our Creator living inside of us.

THE BEAUTY OF WAITING
ON GOD'S TIMING

Life is a journey with paths and navigations,

Sometimes, we want things to happen at a fast pace.

So many thoughts come into our minds about how the future will work,

But, in life, waiting on specific appointed times and God-given moments takes time, patience, and for our character to be built as a person.

God's timing isn't always when we think it is, but when we wait on him, he makes it more beautiful, better, and perfect than we ever thought it could be,

His ways can't always be fathomed, nor his timing, but when we wait on his plan, his timing, and what his true will is, it's more glorious and brings more abundant joy and peace.

ALLOW GOD'S PLAN TO
MOVE IN YOUR LIFE

In life, we all have dreams and desires,

Dreams to become wealthy, famous, and to have a good living.

The desires of our heart, the Almighty knows,

But he has a greater plan for us that is already predestined and set in stone.

But, we must lose our will, desires, and passions in life in order for God to reveal his perfect will for our lives,

When we allow his plans to move in our lives, favor happens that others at times question it.

There's a peace that takes over in our spirit,

When you allow God's plan to move in your life, it allows his true will to be executed and his glory to be seen in your life by others.

His plans and moves in your life are bigger, brighter, and greater than we can ever think or imagine.

STILL HAVING FAITH THROUGH THE ADVERSARY AND ALL ODDS

In this life, many obstacles will try our faith,

Situations will face our faces to see where our true faith lies at.

When breakthroughs, blessings, and changes occur,

Sometimes, adversaries come through people we know really well or even strangers.

That's when you still have faith through the storms,

No matter how it seems on the outside when you keep the faith through all the odds against you.

Walls are brought down, and mountains that tried to keep you from falling,

Begin to move by faith kept during all odds, adversaries, trials, and storms,

It's in the moments of the adversary and all odds that the greatest faith is tested and blessings arrive even more.

THE GOD THAT NEVER STOPS WORKING OR MOVING

It can get hard sometimes walking unknown paths that seem unfamiliar,

It seems cloudy, dark, and filled with confusion when life takes unexpected turns.

When praying to the Lord Jesus, we often think he isn't moving based on our desires and wants,

When we see and look at situations with our natural eyes, discouragement comes.

But we have a mighty Father in heaven that never stops moving,

His ways are higher and glorious.

Just when we think he isn't moving, he shows up at the right time,

He moves in ways never thought of or comprehended with reasoning.

He is the God that moved in ways that keep us in awe of him,

All glory is due to our heavenly Father, who is always on time no matter how it feels or looks.